PIANO

Adventures® *by Nancy and Randall Faber*

A BASIC PIANO METHOD

Aarushi

☑ W9-AZO-438

CONTENTS

Showboat

Middle C Position

Quickly

1 on C?

mf
Come take the riv-er show-boat! Folks, there is real-ly no boat

4 on G?

5

like this old riv-er show-boat trav-'ling down the Mis-sis-sip-pi.

9

Hear how the whis-tle's blow-in', that means we'll soon be go-in'.

13

Last call! Now all a-board the Mis-sis-sip-pi steam-er!

Teacher Duet: (Student plays 1 octave higher)

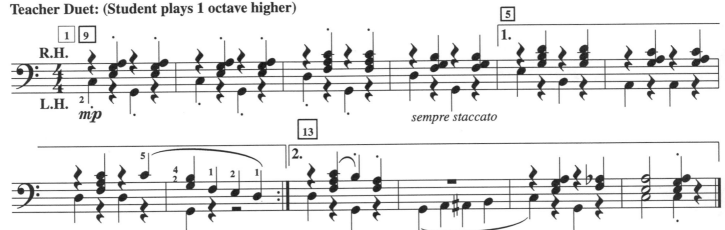

R.H.

L.H. mp

sempre staccato

The Spanish Guitar

Moving along gently

Francesco Molino
(1775-1847, Italy)

DISCOVERY

Point out two ties in this piece to your teacher.

Move to
C Position

Move L.H. to
Middle C Position

Lessons p. 12

3

Jack and the Beanstalk

This piece keeps moving up the piano using the same pattern.
Your teacher will help you with the directions.

With excitement

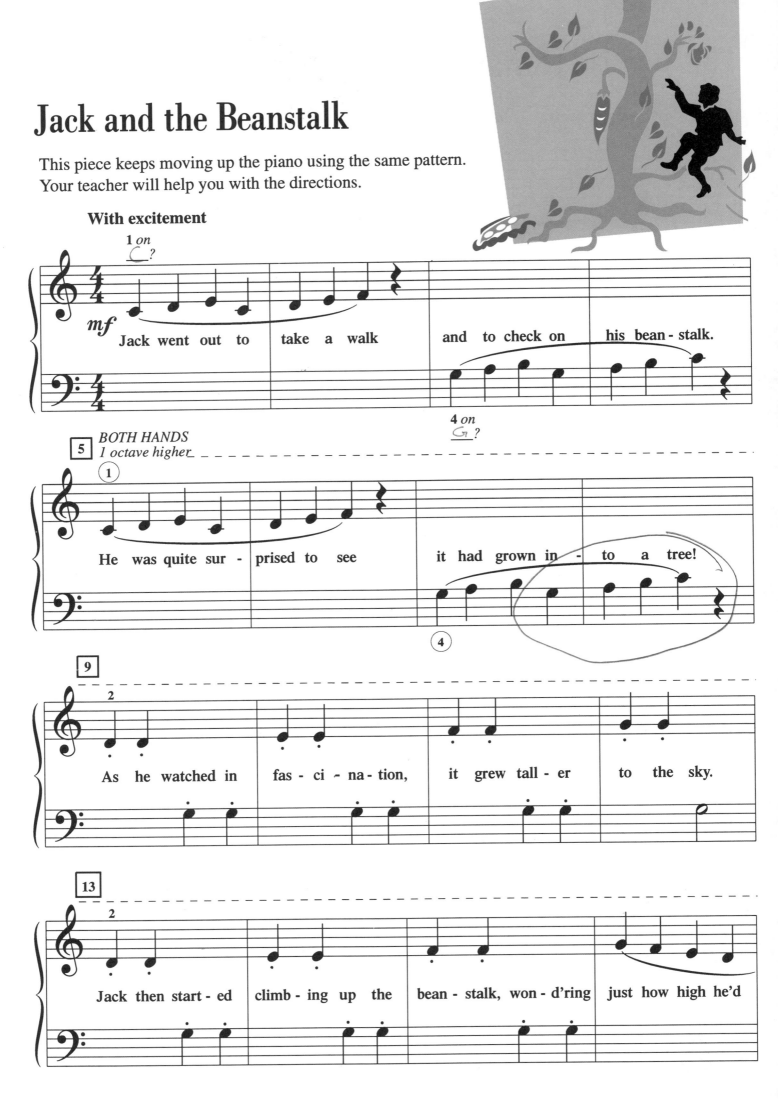

Jack went out to take a walk and to check on his bean - stalk.

He was quite sur - prised to see it had grown in - to a tree!

As he watched in fas - ci - na - tion, it grew tall - er to the sky.

Jack then start - ed climb - ing up the bean - stalk, won - d'ring just how high he'd

17

go if he could reach the top, or per-haps he'd nev-er stop!

21 *BOTH HANDS*
2 octaves higher

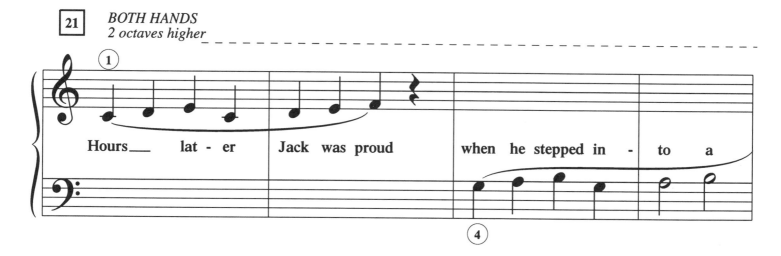

Hours___ lat-er Jack was proud when he stepped in - to a

25

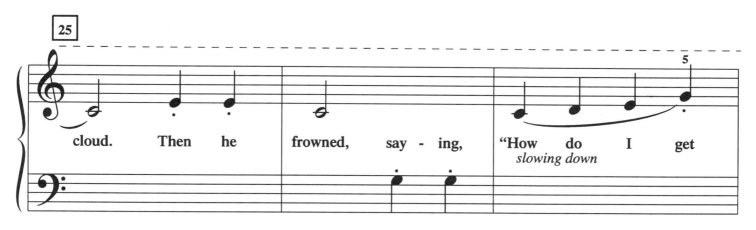

cloud. Then he frowned, say-ing,
slowing down
"How do I get

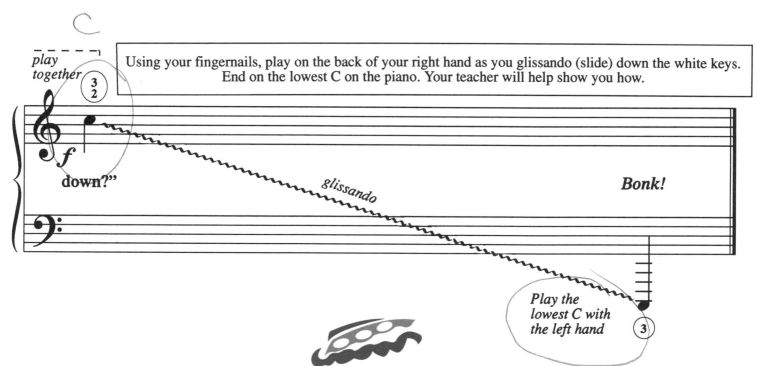

play together

Using your fingernails, play on the back of your right hand as you glissando (slide) down the white keys. End on the lowest C on the piano. Your teacher will help show you how.

f

down?"

glissando

Bonk!

Play the lowest C with the left hand

The Clock Shop

Moderately

Come to the clock shop; you'll hear the tick - tock all day long!

Big clocks and small clocks will tick - tock out their clock song.

Teacher Duet: (Student plays 1 octave higher)

R.H.

L.H. *pp*

mp

pp - mp on repeat

FF

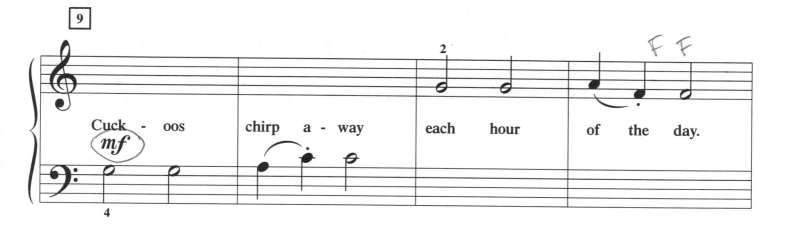

9

Cuck - oos   chirp   a - way   each   hour   of   the   day.

mf

13

Would   you   like   to   hear them   all chime twelve o - clock?   Come on

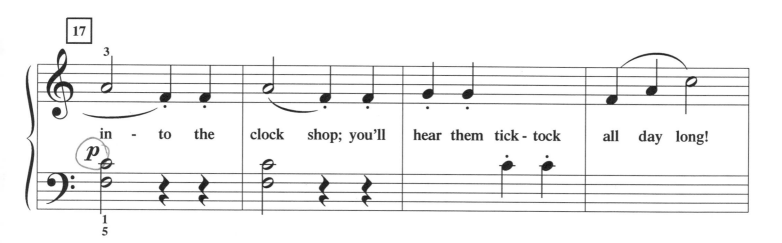

17

in - to   the   clock   shop; you'll   hear them tick - tock   all   day   long!

p

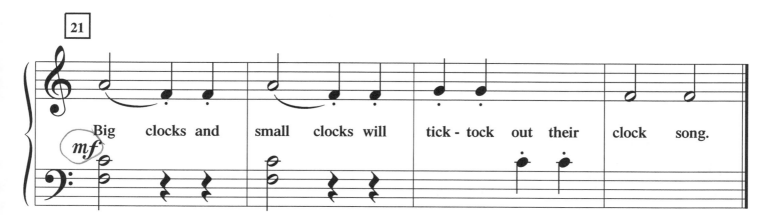

21

Big   clocks and   small   clocks will   tick - tock   out   their   clock   song.

mf

DISCOVERY Where does the music of measures 1-8 return later in the piece?
Show your teacher.

This melody by Beethoven is played in 3 C Positions on the piano:
Bass C, Middle C, and **Treble C Positions.**

Name the L.H. position at *measure 1*, and the
R.H. position at *measure 9* and *measure 17*.

Ode to Joy
(from the *9th Symphony**)

Ludwig van Beethoven
(1770 - 1827, Germany)

Joyfully

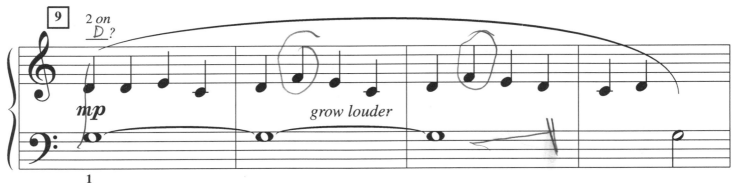

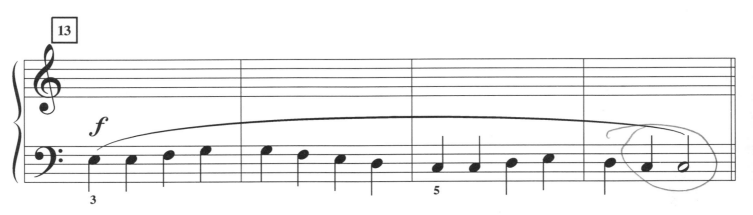

**A symphony is a large-scale work for orchestra. Beethoven, one of the greatest composers of all time,
wrote this symphony after he had gone deaf.*

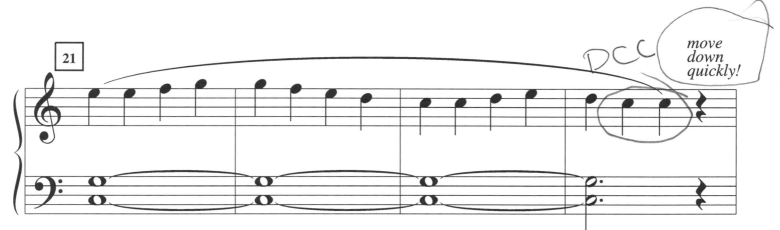

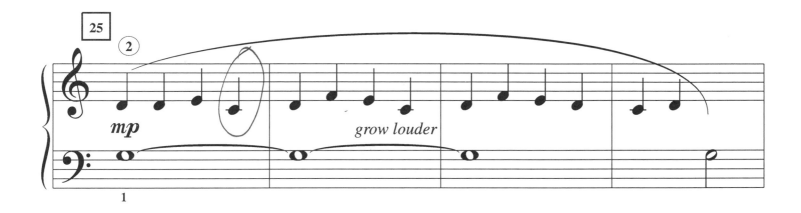

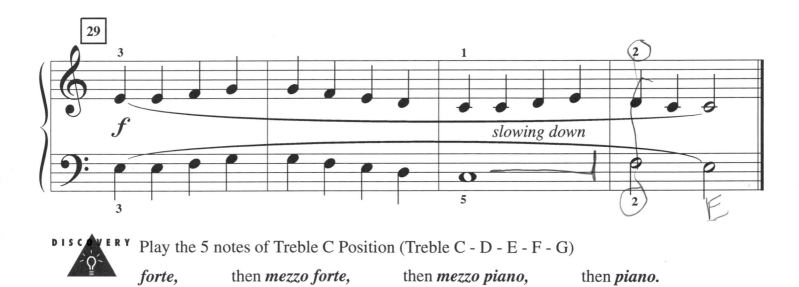

DISCOVERY Play the 5 notes of Treble C Position (Treble C - D - E - F - G)
forte, then *mezzo forte,* then *mezzo piano,* then *piano.*

My Blue Canoe

Painting With Pastels

Hold the right foot pedal down throughout the entire piece.

Gently

My pastels are ready by the easel.

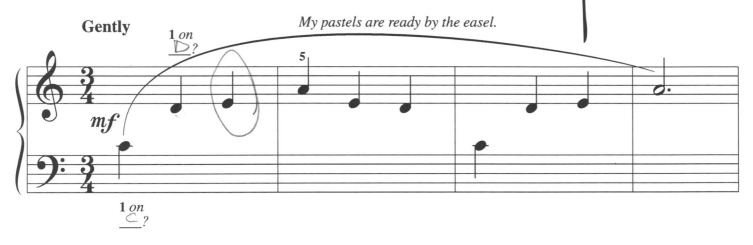

I start to paint   *purples and pinks.*

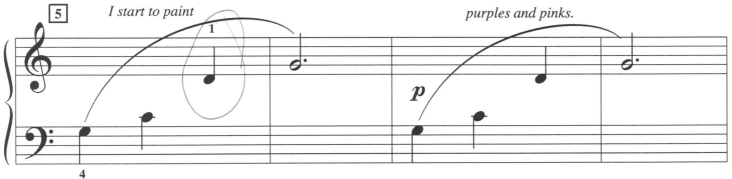

These colors mingle with blues and greens.

When I'm done I'll set it by the window.

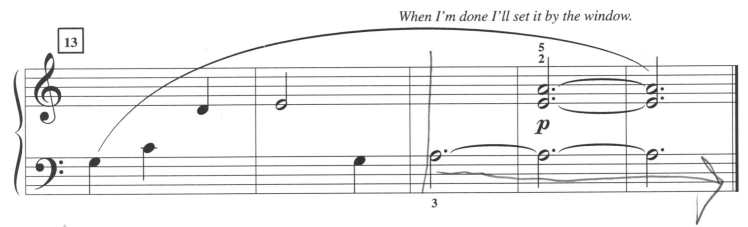

DISCOVERY

Circle each **4th** in this piece. Hint: There are 12.

Lessons p. 22

A Merry March

Cornelius Gurlitt
(1820 - 1901, Germany)

DISCOVERY

Notice that the L.H. has an easy pattern of two notes.
Where does the pattern change to a new note?

Teacher Duet: (Student plays *as written*)

FF

Rusty Old Bike

Squeaking along

DISCOVERY

Circle each **5th** for the R.H. in this piece.

Teacher Duet: (Student plays 1 octave higher)

Before playing, name the intervals in
the boxes given (**2nd, 3rd, 4th, 5th**).

Square Dance

Brightly

5 *on* G ?

f La - dies and gen - tle - men, time to start the show!

1 *on* G ?

5 | 5th | 4th | 3rd | 4th |

In a big old barn, peo - ple gath - er 'round.

mf

9

In their square dance clothes, looks like the whole town.

| 5th | 4th | 3rd | 4th |

13

Fid - dles play - ing mer - ri - ly, what a snap - py tune.

mp

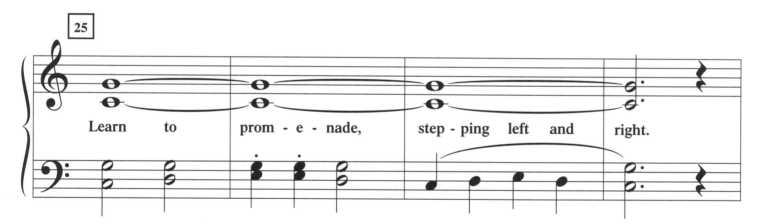

DISCOVERY

Where does the music of measures 5 – 12 return later in the piece?
Your teacher will help you.

The Crazy Clown

Quickly, with mischief

Words by Crystal Bowman

Come and see the cra - zy clown when the cir - cus comes to town.

(prepare L.H.)

R.H. moves quickly

He's so fun - ny, he's so sil - ly, he at - tracts the big - gest crowd.

grow louder

He can jug - gle bright red balls, when he does he al - ways falls.

He's so fun - ny, he's so sil - ly, makes me laugh out loud! Ha!

L.H. gets ready

Play the lowest C on the piano!

D I S C O V E R Y

In which line of music does the R.H. play only half steps? Line ____

Two Little Marches

A Sunny Parade

Rather fast *(Practice slowly at first.)*

Daniel Gottlob Türk
(1756 - 1813, Germany)

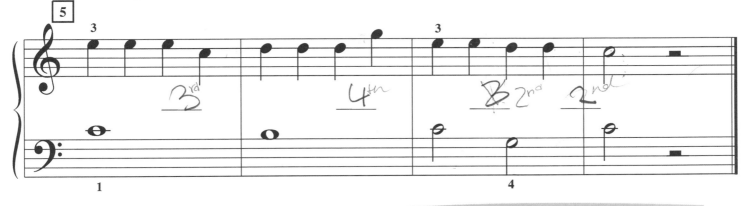

A Rainy Parade

Notice the new hand position.

Rather slowly

DISCOVERY

*In the blanks above, name the interval as a **2nd**, **3rd**, **4th** or **5th**.

The Crawling Spider

Words by Crystal Bowman

FF1

9

Now he spins his web so fine, catch-ing flies for din-ner time.

mp

13

Does this spi-der ev-er sleep, stand-ing on his spin-dly feet?

mf   *f*

F

17

f Spi - der, don't you dare crawl up on my chair.

mp

③

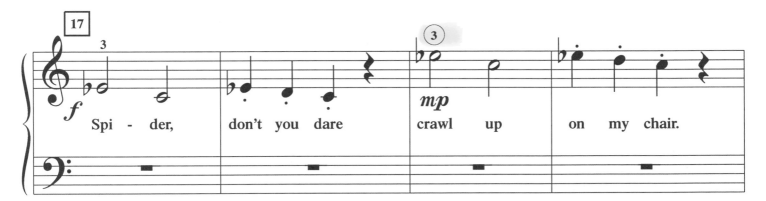

21

8va

Oh no, here he comes! Time for me to run!

p   *f*

③

D I S C O V E R Y

Which two lines of music only have flats (no sharps)? Lines ____ and ____

The Handbell Choir

Secondo - Teacher part

Cornelius Gurlitt (adapted)

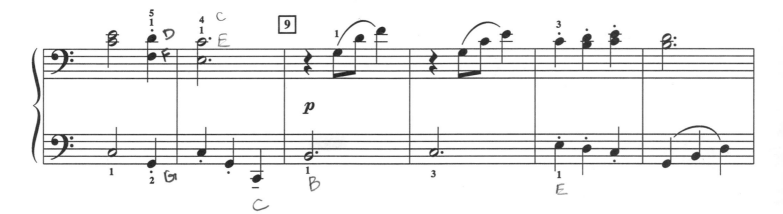

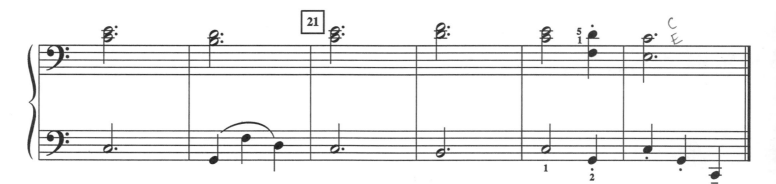

FF

The Handbell Choir

Primo - Student part

Notice that both hands are written in the treble clef.

Cornelius Gurlitt

Not too fast

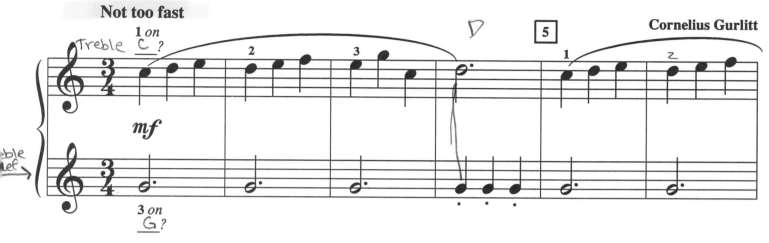

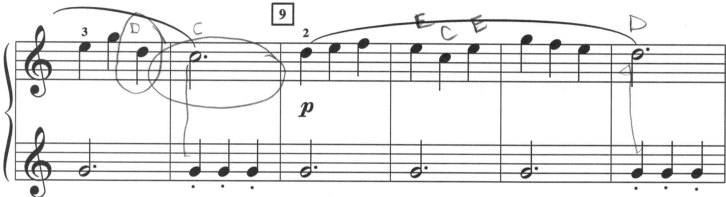

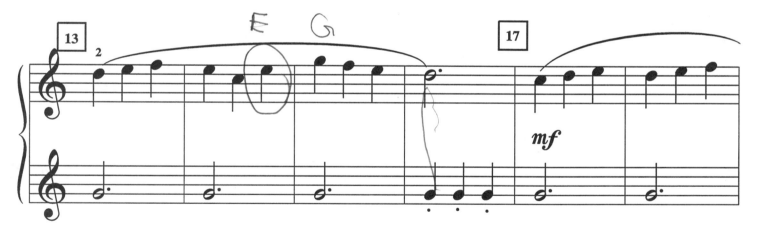

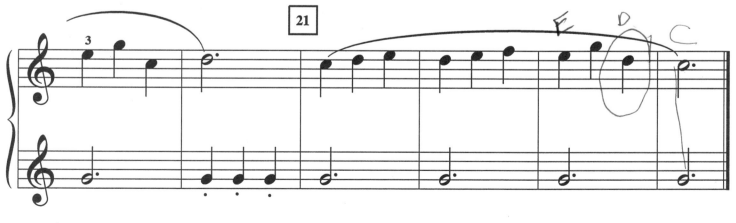

D I S C O V E R Y This piece uses the 5 notes of C Position.

Is the L.H. playing the *tonic* or the *dominant*? (circle the correct answer)

Lessons p. 39

80

21

Miniature Sonatina

A *sonatina* is a piece for piano or other musical instrument that usually has two or three *movements* (parts). Notice that each movement has a character of its own. The performer should pause between movements, and the audience should wait until the end of the sonatina to applaud.

Joseph Kuffner
(1776 - 1856, Germany)
Adapted

First movement

Second movement

Rather slowly

Teacher Duets

First movement - (Student plays 1 octave higher)

Second movement - (Student plays 1 octave higher)

I've Got Music

Moderate beat

I tell my hon - ey
I love to sing it,
I don't have mon - ey,
to sway and swing it.

5 13

but I've got mu - sic down in my soul.
Yes, I've got mu - sic down in my soul.

Teacher Duet: (Student plays 1 octave higher)

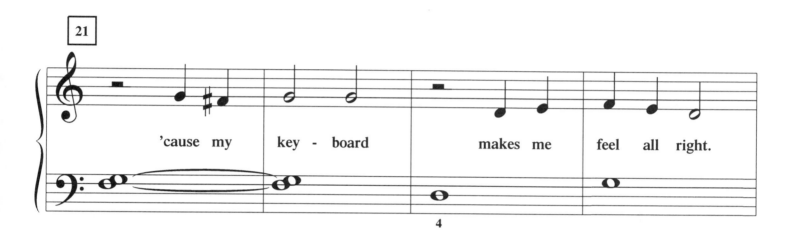

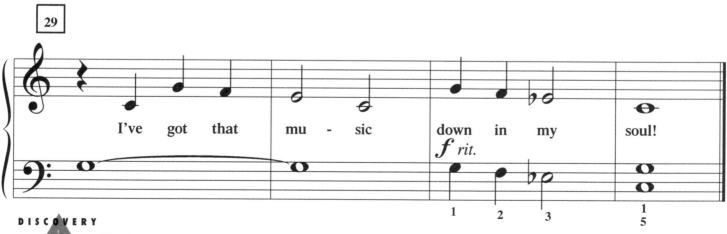

DISCOVERY

Circle each V7 chord in this piece.

UNIT

Rain Dance

G Position

With a strong beat

mf

f

FF

DISCOVERY The L.H. plays only tonic and dominant notes. True / False (circle one)

Sound Check: Circle all the dynamic marks.
Listen to your dynamics as you play.

Bells! Bells! Bells! 7/15

Hold the right foot (damper) pedal down throughout the entire piece.

Moderately fast

1 *on* G ?

1 *on* D ?

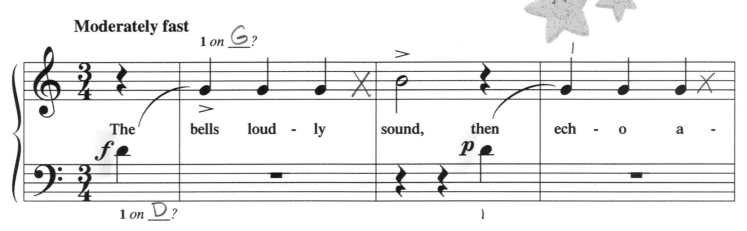

The   bells   loud - ly   sound,   then   ech - o   a -

f   *p*

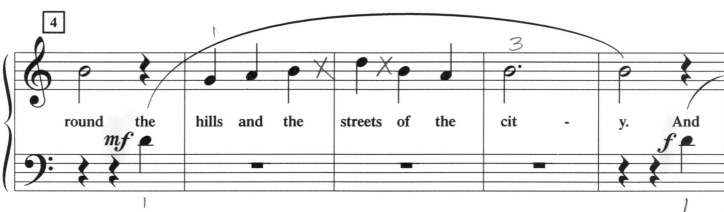

round   the   hills   and   the   streets   of   the   cit - y.   And

mf   *f*

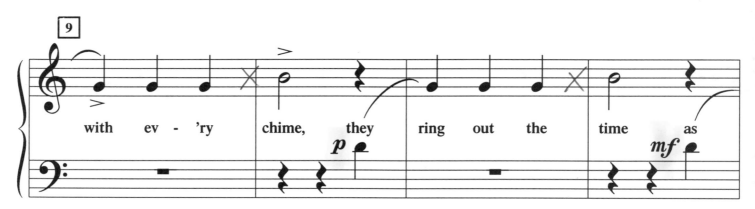

with   ev - 'ry   chime,   they   ring   out   the   time   as

p   *mf*

morn - ing   a - wakes   in   the   cit - y.

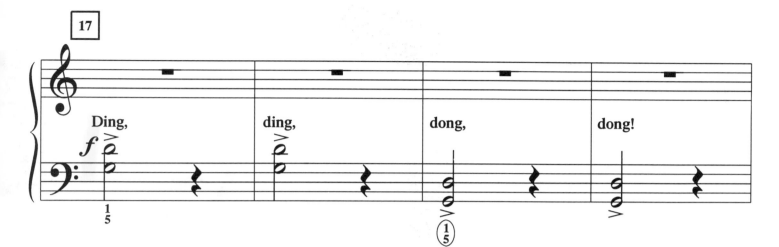

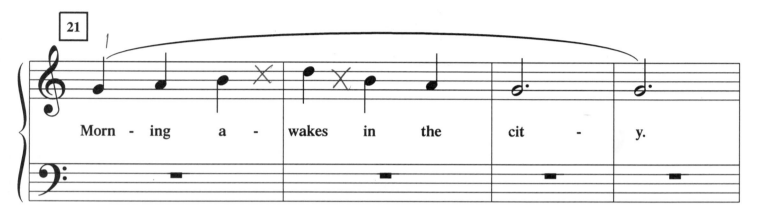

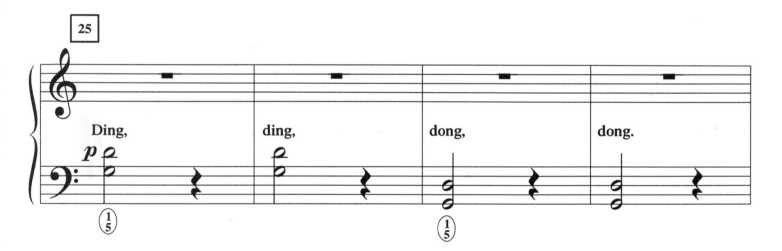

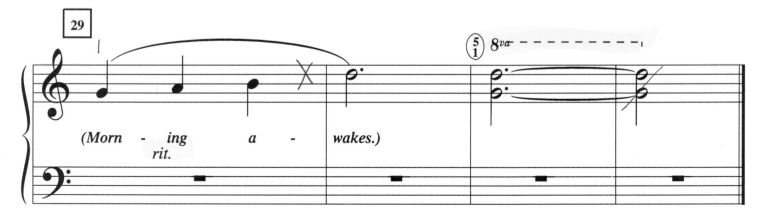

DISCOVERY

Does this piece begin on **beat 1, beat 2,** or **beat 3?** *(circle one)*

The San Francisco Trolley

Name the position. G

Sounding busy

5 *on* D?
1 *on* G?

p

gradually play louder

5 *on* G?

1   2   1

5

f

5

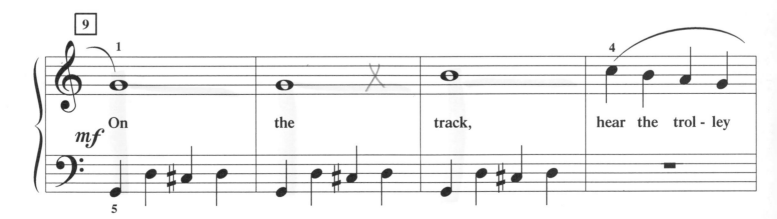

9

mf   On   the   track,   hear the trol - ley

5

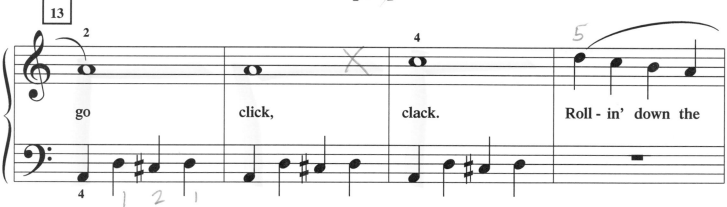

go click, clack. Roll - in' down the

cit - y streets, rid - in' on the

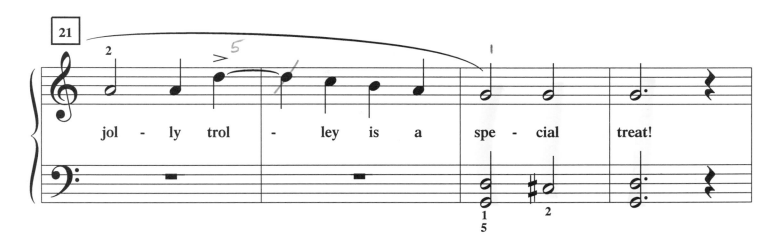

jol - ly trol - ley is a spe - cial treat!

gradually play softer
rit.

𝒑

DISCOVERY At the beginning of this piece, is the trolley getting closer or farther away?
Tell your teacher.

Sound Check: Can you play the chords *softer* than the melody?

Apple Tree Waltz

Rather slowly

Ap - ples sway - ing,

Wind in the branch - es is play - ing.

Swing - ing, sway - ing,

Won't you climb up and play, too? *rit.*

1 on D?

Teacher Duet: (Student plays 1 octave higher)

R.H.

L.H. *mp* *with pedal*

1.

2.

rit.

FF